MW01448268

INSIDE THE NBA

LOS ANGELES LAKERS

BY PATRICK DONNELLY

SportsZone

An Imprint of Abdo Publishing
abdobooks.com

abdobooks.com

Published by Abdo Publishing, a division of ABDO, PO Box 398166, Minneapolis, Minnesota 55439.

Printed in the United States of America, North Mankato, Minnesota.
052022
092022

Cover Photo: Ringo H.W. Chiu/AP Images
Interior Photos: Melinda Nagy/Shutterstock Images, 1; Kevin C. Cox/Getty Images Sport/Getty Images, 4, 6, 7; Mark J. Terrill/AP Images, 9, 11, 21; AP Photo, 12; Bettmann/Getty Images, 15, 22, 32; Focus on Sport/Getty Images, 17, 25, 27, 34, 37; Mark Lennihan/AP Images, 18; John Ruthoff/AFP/Getty Images, 20; Tony Tomsic/AP Images, 24; Stephen Dunn/Getty Images Sport/Getty Images, 29; Kevork Djansezian/Getty Images Sport/Getty Images, 31; Lisa Blumenfeld/Getty Images Sport/Getty Images, 38; Harry How/Getty Images Sport/Getty Images, 41

Editor: Charlie Beattie
Series Designer: Joshua Olson

Library of Congress Control Number: 2021951662

Publisher's Cataloging-in-Publication Data

Names: Donnelly, Patrick, author.
Title: Los Angeles Lakers / by Patrick Donnelly
Description: Minneapolis, Minnesota: Abdo Publishing, 2023 | Series: Inside the NBA | Includes online resources and index.
Identifiers: ISBN 9781532198311 (lib. bdg.) | ISBN 9781098271961 (ebook)
Subjects: LCSH: Los Angeles Lakers (Basketball team)--Juvenile literature. | Basketball--Juvenile literature. | Professional sports--Juvenile literature. | Sports franchises--Juvenile literature.
Classification: DDC 796.32364--dc23

TABLE OF CONTENTS

wish
LAKERS
23

CHAPTER ONE

KING JAMES HOLDS COURT

In a normal National Basketball Association (NBA) season, most teams are just starting preseason training camp in October. But the 2019–20 season was anything but ordinary. NBA teams stopped playing in March 2020. The season was suspended when the COVID-19 pandemic began sweeping through North America. Play resumed in late July with all teams isolated from the public in a "bubble" at the Walt Disney World Resort near Orlando, Florida.

Even in these unique circumstances, the Los Angeles Lakers ended the season in a familiar position. After nearly three months in the bubble, forward LeBron James led the Lakers to the NBA Finals. And on October 11, they took the court to face the Miami Heat. The NBA's strangest season was coming to an end. On this night, the NBA title was on the line.

LeBron James was looking to win an NBA title with his third team in 2020.

PROVEN WINNER

The Lakers were leading the Western Conference when the pandemic hit. They held on to the top seed in the West when the playoffs began in mid-August. Los Angeles cruised through the first three rounds, losing just three games along the way. Center Anthony Davis was the team's leading scorer and rebounder in the regular season. He continued his dominance in the playoffs. Role players Kentavious Caldwell-Pope, Rajon Rondo, and Kyle Kuzma made important contributions. But if the Lakers were going to bring home their seventeenth NBA title, everyone knew they would lean on James when the going got tough.

James averaged 25.2 points, 7.8 rebounds, and a team-high 10.2 assists for the Lakers in 2019–20.

James arrived in Los Angeles in July 2018. It seemed like a perfect match between an elite player and a storied franchise. James had won two NBA titles with the Miami Heat and another

Anthony Davis led the Lakers in scoring and rebounding during the 2019–20 season.

with the Cleveland Cavaliers. The Lakers had won 16 NBA championships. That was one shy of the Boston Celtics for the all-time record. But Los Angeles had missed the playoffs for five straight seasons. Needing a superstar, the Lakers looked in James's direction for a change in fortunes.

However, James's first season in Los Angeles was a disaster. James and many of his teammates struggled with injuries in 2018–19. James missed 27 games that year. He sat for the final six when the team shut him down for the season with a strained groin. The Lakers missed the postseason again.

Los Angeles's general manager, Rob Pelinka, wasn't done retooling the roster. That offseason he traded for Davis. The center was a six-time All-Star with the New Orleans Pelicans. And he was still only 25 when the 2019–20 season started.

Davis and James proved to be a great combination. James could focus more on his all-around game while Davis shouldered more of the scoring and rebounding load.

It didn't take long for the Lakers to get results. By the end of November, they were 17–2 and running away with the Western Conference. They responded to a four-game skid in mid-December by immediately winning nine straight.

When the season was suspended on March 12, the Lakers were 49–14. They led the West by five and a half games. When the season resumed, every team played eight games inside the bubble to help determine playoff seeding. The Lakers went only 3–5 over that stretch as they worked to regain their form. It was still good enough to clinch the number one seed in the Western Conference.

PLAYOFF POWERHOUSE

The Lakers lost the opening game in each of their first two playoff series, against the Portland Trail Blazers and Houston Rockets. But in both cases, Los Angeles swept the next four games to move on.

The Denver Nuggets awaited in the Western Conference Finals. This time, the Lakers won the first two before Denver notched a victory in Game 3. But once again the Lakers closed out the series in five, with James posting a triple-double (38 points, 16 rebounds, 10 assists) in the clincher.

The Lakers were on a roll. Few thought the Eastern Conference would provide much competition in the NBA Finals. The top four seeds all fell in the early rounds. The fifth-seeded Miami Heat scored three straight upsets to reach the Finals. But their luck would be tested against Los Angeles.

James watches a shot during Game 5 of the Lakers' 2020 playoff series with the Denver Nuggets.

When the Lakers won three of the first four games, another five-game wipeout was a possibility. But the Heat rallied to win Game 5. Star forward Jimmy Butler put up a triple-double of his own. If the Heat could do it again in Game 6, it would all come down to one final game for the NBA title. The Lakers wanted to do anything they could to avoid that much drama.

PUTTING IT AWAY

James didn't waste any time getting on the stat sheet. On the first trip down the court, he found Davis for an open jumper.

Davis then stole the ball, and James streaked out behind the Heat defense. He took a pass from Alex Caruso in stride and threw down a powerful dunk.

Time and again, James attacked the basket. He slithered through two or three defenders on the way to the hoop. And when he found it a bit too crowded, James passed to teammates who had open shots.

The Lakers pulled out to a double-digit lead in the second quarter. James found Caldwell-Pope for a basket. Then James slid a bounce pass to Caruso for a layup. Once again James set up Caldwell-Pope, this time for a three-pointer from the corner. By halftime, James had 11 points, nine rebounds, and six assists, and the Lakers had surged to a 64–36 lead.

The Lakers cruised in the second half. James finished with 28 points, 14 rebounds, and 10 assists. Out of the four series-clinching games the Lakers had won in the postseason,

Tripling Up on Triple-Doubles

James was no stranger to big performances in championship-clinching games. In the decisive Game 5 of the 2012 Finals with the Miami Heat, James put up 26 points, 11 rebounds, and 13 assists. In 2016 he did it again. That year James put up a 27-point, 11-rebound, 11-assist performance as his hometown Cleveland Cavaliers defeated the Golden State Warriors in Game 7.

The Lakers hoist the NBA championship trophy after defeating the Heat 106–93 in Game 6 of the 2020 NBA Finals.

James had earned triple doubles in three of them. The Lakers poured off the bench to mob James as the final buzzer sounded. Los Angeles had tied the Boston Celtics by winning its seventeenth NBA title with a 106–93 victory over Miami.

After the game, Lakers coach Frank Vogel paid James the ultimate compliment. "I have always believed in LeBron James," Vogel said. "He's the greatest player the basketball universe has ever seen."

LAKERS
99

CHAPTER TWO

A HISTORY OF DYNASTIES

In 1947 the Detroit Gems of the National Basketball League (NBL) were finished. The team had gone 4–40 the year before and was about to fold. Two businessmen from Minnesota stepped in and bought the team. They moved the Gems to Minneapolis and renamed them the Lakers. It was a reference to Minnesota as the "land of 10,000 lakes." But there was one problem—the new Lakers had no players. Everyone who played for the Detroit Gems had been let go.

The new owners caught a big break, however. A rival professional league folded that year. The NBL held a draft to distribute the new players. Because the Gems were the worst team in the league, the Lakers got the first pick. Center George Mikan was the obvious choice.

Mikan was basketball's first big star. He dominated from his center position. And the Lakers quickly surrounded him with

The Minneapolis Lakers put head coach John Kundla on their shoulders after winning the 1952 NBA title.

other talented players. They won the NBL championship in 1947–48. Then they were lured away from NBL by another rival league, the Basketball Association of America (BAA). The Lakers won the title in their first BAA season too.

Rule Changer

In the early days of the NBA, games were played without a shot clock. On November 22, 1950, the Fort Wayne Pistons decided to hold the ball for minutes at a time to keep the ball away from the dominant Lakers. Fort Wayne won the game 19–18, the lowest score ever in an NBA game. The league addressed such slowdown tactics by adding a shot clock in 1954.

Finally, before the 1949–50 season, the BAA and NBL merged to become the NBA. The Lakers were its first dynasty. They won again that season. It was their third championship in their third league in three years. Minneapolis defeated the Syracuse Nationals 4–2 in the first official NBA Finals. Mikan averaged 32.2 points per game to lead the way.

The next season, the Lakers were upset in the semifinals. But they bounced back and conquered the NBA each of the next three years. Coach John Kundla's Lakers leaned heavily on Mikan. But they had three other future Hall of Famers on the roster. Point guard Slater Martin, small forward Jim Pollard, and power forward Vern Mikkelsen were key contributors to the Lakers' success.

Elgin Baylor (22) glides to the basket against the Cincinnati Royals in 1962.

GO WEST

By the end of the 1955–56 season, Mikan, Pollard, and Martin had all retired or been traded away. As the team's core players left, the Lakers struggled to stay on top. They also struggled to draw fans. Rock bottom came in 1957–58, when Minneapolis finished 19–53. But that gave the Lakers the top pick in the draft. They used it to select forward Elgin Baylor.

Baylor immediately energized the Lakers. He won the Rookie of the Year award and led the team back to the NBA Finals. But after one more mediocre season, the Lakers were gone. Owner Robert Short saw professional football and baseball thriving in Los Angeles. He decided to move the Lakers there in 1960.

That same year, the Lakers added another Hall of Famer. Point guard Jerry West arrived as the second overall pick of the 1960 draft. He and Baylor established Los Angeles as the dominant team in the Western Division. They reached the NBA Finals seven times in nine years.

Close Call

The Lakers' move to Los Angeles in 1960 was almost derailed by tragedy. In January of that year, the team plane had to make an emergency landing in an Iowa cornfield during a snowstorm. The Lakers were returning from a game in St. Louis when the plane's electronics failed. The plane veered off course. It was over western Iowa when the crew realized they were low on fuel. With the windshield frosted over, the pilot, Harold Gifford, stuck his head out the window to scrape off the ice. He then guided the plane down onto a snow-packed field. Amazingly, no one was injured.

Winning another title, however, proved to be a bigger challenge. The Boston Celtics were in the middle of the best dynasty in NBA history. Six times in the 1960s, the Lakers lost to Boston in the Finals. Their final meeting, in 1969, went seven games. West scored 42 points in Game 7. Newly acquired center Wilt Chamberlain grabbed 27 rebounds. But Boston pulled out a 108–106 victory.

The Lakers lost the Finals again the next season, this time to the New York Knicks. It was another heartbreaking seven-game series. Fans wondered if the Lakers' day would ever come again.

The 1971–72 Lakers are widely regarded as one of the best teams the NBA has ever seen. Baylor was limited to just nine games in his final season. But West and Chamberlain played like All-Stars. Flashy guard Gail Goodrich and sturdy forward Jim McMillan played huge roles as well. Los Angeles won 33 straight games on its way to a 69–13 record. Then the Lakers coasted through the playoffs. They capped off the run by routing the Knicks 4–1 in the Finals.

Jerry West was the Lakers' all-time leader in games played and points scored when he retired in 1974.

SHOWTIME

In 1975 the Lakers missed the playoffs for the first time since they had moved to Los Angeles. That summer they made a trade with the Milwaukee Bucks to acquire Kareem Abdul-Jabbar. The 7-foot-2-inch center was already a star. He was the first piece of the Lakers' next dynasty.

In 1976 Goodrich left the Lakers and joined the New Orleans Jazz. As compensation, the Lakers received four draft picks,

Magic Johnson (32) attacks the Boston Celtics' defense during a game in 1987.

including New Orleans' first-rounder in 1979. Losing a star like Goodrich hurt. But it turned out to be the best thing to happen to the Lakers. When the 1979 draft pick came around, it was the number one overall selection. The Lakers used it on a 6-foot-9-inch point guard from Michigan State University. His name was Earvin "Magic" Johnson.

With Johnson and Abdul-Jabbar leading the way, the Lakers went on a tear. They won five NBA titles between 1980 and

1988. And they did it with style. Johnson's no-look passes and fast-break skills entertained fans from coast to coast. Lakers games became known as "Showtime." Celebrities flocked to the Forum, the Lakers' home arena. In a city filled with movie stars, Lakers games became the place to be seen.

The decade also rekindled the matchup between the Lakers and Celtics. The teams met in the Finals three times during the 1980s. Boston won the first meeting in 1984. But the Lakers finally got the better of their cross-country rivals by winning in both 1985 and 1987.

THE LAKE SHOW

In the 1991 NBA Finals, the aging Lakers passed the baton to Michael Jordan's Chicago Bulls. It was the end of Los Angeles's run at the top. In 1993–94 the team missed the playoffs completely. It took another smart trade and a big free-agent signing to turn things around.

In July 1996, the Lakers traded for 18-year-old guard Kobe Bryant. Later that month, Los Angeles announced the signing of former Orlando Magic center Shaquille O'Neal. Over the next few seasons, Los Angeles built smartly around its two new stars. And in 1999 the Lakers added a legendary coach. Phil Jackson came out of a brief retirement to take over.

Jackson had twice won three straight NBA titles with the Bulls in the 1990s. He did it again in his first three years with the dominant Lakers. In 2000 they knocked off the Indiana Pacers in six games for a title. The next year the Philadelphia 76ers were no match in a five-game Lakers victory. A four-game Finals sweep of the New Jersey Nets followed in 2002.

Kobe Bryant (8) and Shaquille O'Neal (34) didn't always get along, but they won three straight NBA titles together in the early 2000s.

It seemed like there were no other teams that could bring down the Lakers. But in the end, the Lakers brought down themselves. Both O'Neal and Bryant saw themselves as the team's top dog. The always-rocky relationship between the two had fallen apart by 2004. O'Neal was traded to the Miami Heat. It was now Bryant's time to shine.

The Bryant era sputtered at first. The Lakers didn't win a playoff series the first three seasons without O'Neal. Bryant finally got another ring in 2009 as the Lakers knocked off the Magic in the Finals. He added another the next year, edging the Celtics in seven games.

LeBron James delivered the Lakers their seventeenth NBA championship in 2020, matching the Celtics for the most in league history.

That was the career peak for Bryant. He suffered a torn Achilles tendon in April 2013. He injured his leg when he returned to action in December. That injury sidelined him for the rest of the 2013–14 season. A variety of injuries hampered him the rest of his career. He retired in 2016.

Without their star, the Lakers struggled. They missed the playoffs six straight seasons. But the arrival of forward LeBron James and center Anthony Davis helped the Lakers reach the top again in 2020. Fans hoped it would be the start of the latest Lakers dynasty.

LAKERS
99

CHAPTER THREE

LEGENDARY LAKERS

In 1950 George Mikan was voted the greatest basketball player in the first half of the twentieth century. He had been playing professionally for only four years. The sport's first superstar won scoring titles and championships in three different professional leagues before he retired. Mikan was so dominant that he prompted rule changes. Goaltending was outlawed in college basketball because Mikan blocked so many shots while starring for DePaul University. Later, the NBA widened the lane from six to 12 feet (1.8 m to 3.7 m) to keep big men from camping out near the basket.

Mikan led the Lakers to one BAA and three NBA titles, but he had plenty of help. Vern Mikkelsen is credited with pioneering the position of power forward. At 6 feet, 7 inches and 230 pounds, Mikkelsen was strong and sturdy. Few teams had enough size to match up with Mikan and Mikkelsen. It got

George Mikan led the league in scoring three times and rebounding twice during his seven-year NBA career.

Jerry West was an All-Star in all 14 of his NBA seasons.

even harder for opponents when 6-foot-9-inch forward Clyde Lovellette joined the team in 1953.

Minneapolis could also play outside. Forward Jim Pollard was nicknamed "the Kangaroo Kid" because of his leaping ability. He also was a reliable outside shot. Slater Martin helped define the point guard position with his passing and scrappy defense.

THE LOGO

Elgin Baylor was the Lakers' last link to their original home. He played two years in Minneapolis before the team moved to Los Angeles. Baylor was a 6-foot-5-inch flash with great leaping ability. He became the first NBA player to score 70 points in a game.

Baylor played a huge role in the Lakers' dominance of the Western Division. So did guard Jerry West. The West Virginia native was a 14-time All-Star. He could dominate the game

Kareem Abdul-Jabbar, *left*, broke the All-time NBA scoring record while wearing a Lakers uniform in 1984.

as both a passer and a scorer. West is one of the most iconic players in NBA history—literally. The league's logo is believed to be patterned after a silhouette of West dribbling.

West and Baylor got a big boost when center Wilt Chamberlain arrived in 1968. "The Big Dipper" was already one of the game's biggest stars. He and high-scoring guard Gail Goodrich helped the Lakers finally win their first title in Los Angeles in 1972.

Visionary Owner

Jerry Buss had a vision. When he purchased the Lakers in 1979, Buss knew the NBA had the potential to be more than just a sports league. He turned Lakers games into spectacles. Buss gave courtside seats to movie stars. He also hired the glamorous Laker Girls dance team to entertain the crowd. The team's Showtime reputation owed as much to Buss as it did to its star players. When he died in 2013, his daughter Jeanie became the team's controlling owner.

STARS OF SHOWTIME

Kareem Abdul-Jabbar was the NBA's top center in the 1970s and '80s. He joined the Lakers in a 1975 trade from the Milwaukee Bucks. Abdul-Jabbar was right at home in Los Angeles, where he had starred in college at UCLA. He won three Most Valuable Player (MVP) trophies with the Lakers, using his trademark skyhook to become the league's all-time leading scorer.

It didn't hurt that he played with the most creative point guard in the league. Magic Johnson was the engine that drove coach Pat Riley's "Showtime" Lakers to greatness. His quick outlet passes to the likes of forwards Jamaal Wilkes and James Worthy kick-started the team's lethal transition game.

Magic Johnson throws one of his signature no-look passes.

Those star players led the Lakers to five titles in the 1980s. Important role players included scrappy forward Kurt Rambis and outside shooter Byron Scott. Guard Michael Cooper was a five-time member of the NBA All-Defensive first team. Norm Nixon shared point guard duties on the first two title teams, allowing Johnson more freedom to get creative.

Johnson shocked the world when he announced his retirement in November 1991. He had been diagnosed with human immunodeficiency virus (HIV). In those days, HIV was generally viewed as a death sentence. But Johnson went on to prove that with proper treatment, people can be HIV-positive and lead healthy lives. He returned to coach the Lakers briefly in 1994. Johnson then came back to the court for one last hurrah as a player, suiting up for 32 regular-season and four playoff games in 1996.

SHAQ, KOBE, AND THE KING

The Lakers' next two superstars joined the team the same year Johnson left for good. Shaquille O'Neal towered over opponents. But the 7-foot-1-inch, 325-pound center was surprisingly nimble for a man his size. And he had a big personality to match his massive frame. Off the court, O'Neal dabbled in just about everything from acting to music to law enforcement. But no outside interest kept him from putting together a winning career.

Kobe Bryant went straight from high school to the bright lights of the NBA. In 1997–98, his second season, Bryant earned the first of his 18 All-Star nods. He was often viewed as an heir to Michael Jordan's title as the league's best all-around player. Bryant strove to meet those expectations. He was an elite scorer and dominant defender. Early in his career, he was seen as somewhat of a selfish player. But by the time he retired, the player known as "Black Mamba" had earned league-wide respect. When he died tragically in a helicopter crash in January 2020, Bryant was honored by nearly every team in the NBA.

Kobe Bryant smashed Jerry West's Lakers' scoring record by over 8,000 points.

Under head coach Phil Jackson, Bryant and O'Neal won three straight NBA titles from 1999–2000 to 2001–02. They got plenty of help from sturdy point guard Derek Fisher and versatile forward Rick Fox. Meanwhile, forward Robert Horry earned the nickname "Big Shot Rob" thanks to his knack for clutch scoring.

Bryant led the Lakers to two more titles, in 2009 and 2010, ensuring his legacy as one of the game's all-time greats. With O'Neal gone, the Lakers relied on a large group of supporting stars. Power forward Pau Gasol averaged close to a double-double on both championship teams. Center Andrew Bynum followed Bryant's high-school-to-NBA path. He was a reliable scorer and rebounder. Forward Lamar Odom filled the stat sheet with his versatility.

Jerry West Coast

Jerry West spent most of his life as a Laker. After he retired from playing, he led the team to three playoff appearances as head coach. He then spent time as a scout before taking over as general manager in 1982. Under his management, the Lakers won six titles before he finally left the team in 2002.

Another of the NBA's greatest players wrote a few chapters of his life story with the Lakers. LeBron James had already won three championships and four NBA MVP Awards before he arrived in Los Angeles in 2018. He was always a great scorer. But in 2019–20, James proved his playmaking ability. His 10.2 assists per game led the NBA for the first time in his career.

That year the Lakers acquired center Anthony Davis from New Orleans. He gave the team a much-needed defensive presence. Davis also averaged 27.7 points during the 2020 playoffs. He and James led the Lakers to their seventeenth NBA title.

Anthony Davis's arrival in 2019 helped make the Lakers NBA champions again.

99
FT. WAYNE
9
17
12

CHAPTER FOUR

SHOWTIME

In the spring of 1950, the newly formed NBA was looking to crown its champion. The Minneapolis Lakers were cochampions of the Central Division with a 51–17 record. They reached the finals against the Syracuse Nationals.

The Nationals were led by a front line of Dolph Schayes, Ed Peterson, and Alex Hannum. All three players were at least 6 feet, 7 inches tall.

But the Lakers had a stacked lineup with plenty of size too. Center George Mikan was the new league's biggest star. And rookie power forward Vern Mikkelsen was already showing his Hall-of-Fame skills.

In Game 1, Lakers reserve guard Bob "Tiger" Harrison got the ball near half-court with three seconds left in a 66–66 tie. He took two dribbles and launched a set shot that swished through the hoop as the buzzer sounded.

George Mikan (99) goes up for a layup against the Fort Wayne Zollner Pistons in 1956.

Wilt Chamberlain averaged 14.8 points and an NBA-best 19.2 rebounds per game during Los Angeles's 1971–72 championship run.

The Lakers took two of the next four games, setting up Game 6 at the Minneapolis Auditorium. Mikan, who led the NBA in scoring at 27.4 points per game, made sure the series wouldn't return to Syracuse for Game 7. He exploded for 40 points as the Lakers built a 25-point lead. Minneapolis rolled to a 110–95 victory. It was the Lakers' third title in three leagues in three years. It set the stage for three more NBA titles in the next four seasons.

STREAKING TO A TITLE

Forward Elgin Baylor and guard Jerry West led the team to seven Western Division titles between 1962 and 1970. However, they went 0-for-7 in the NBA Finals. They lost six in a row to the Boston Celtics and a seventh against the New York Knicks.

All the pieces finally fell into place in 1971–72. On November 5 the Lakers defeated the Baltimore Bullets 110–106. The win ran Los Angeles's record to 7–3. It was the start of a historic run. They were perfect through November and again through December. Los Angeles didn't lose again until January 9. That day the Lakers fell to the Milwaukee Bucks 120–104 on the road. The 33-game winning

Setting the Bar

The Lakers' 33-game winning streak in 1971–72 is one of the league's most hallowed records. The closest any team has come to matching it was when the Golden State Warriors won 28 straight in 2015. The Warriors' streak started in the 2014–15 season and ended in 2015–16. The longest single-season streak since the Lakers' mark came in 2012–13 when the Miami Heat won 27 in a row.

streak broke the NBA record of 20, established by the Bucks a year earlier.

The Lakers rode that momentum to a 69–13 record. At the time, that was the most wins any NBA team had ever earned in the regular season. And their success continued into the playoffs. In a second-round series against the Bucks, center Wilt Chamberlain and future Laker Kareem Abdul-Jabbar waged a battle inside. Abdul-Jabbar averaged 33.7 points and 17.5 rebounds. But the aging Chamberlain held his own. He scored 20 points and grabbed 24 boards in Game 6. The Lakers won 104–100 in Milwaukee to clinch the series.

The Finals gave the Lakers another chance at revenge when they once again faced the Knicks. This time, it was no contest. After losing Game 1, the Lakers swept the next four to finally give Los Angeles an NBA championship. Chamberlain was named the series MVP after averaging 19.4 points and 23.2 rebounds.

THE MAGIC HOUR

When the 1979–80 season began, the Lakers were still searching for their second title in Los Angeles. Abdul-Jabbar had been a Laker for four years, but the closest the team had come was a loss in the Western Conference finals in 1977.

Those teams didn't have Magic Johnson. The 20-year-old point guard took the league by storm when he arrived in 1979.

Magic Johnson, *left*, scoops in a layup against the Philadelphia 76ers in the 1980 NBA Finals.

His enthusiasm and skill won over fans immediately. The rookie averaged 18.0 points, 7.7 rebounds, and 7.3 assists per game.

The Lakers reached the NBA Finals. They took a 3–2 lead over the Philadelphia 76ers behind Abdul-Jabbar's 33.4 points

Kobe Bryant scored at least 60 points in a single game six times in his career.

per game. But Los Angeles had a big problem. Abdul-Jabbar sprained his ankle in Game 5. He wouldn't be available for Game 6 back in Philadelphia.

Johnson was there to save the day. He told the team, "Never fear, E. J. is here!" Then he stepped into Abdul-Jabbar's spot at center. Johnson had never played the position in his life, but he proceeded to dominate. Johnson scored 42 points, grabbed 15 rebounds, and dished out seven assists. His epic performance led the Lakers to a 123–107 victory. Johnson was named the series MVP.

His coach, Paul Westhead, was one of the few people in the arena who wasn't surprised by what he had just seen. "Our Magical Man, our Houdini," Westhead said. "But the move to center really wasn't as strange as it seemed. We knew Magic would present problems for them, and he did."

KOBE'S TRIUMPH AND TRAGEDY

Chamberlain's 100-point performance against the Knicks on March 2, 1962, is the stuff of legend. Through 2005, nobody had come within 27 points of matching it. His own 78-point game in 1961 was second on the single-game scoring list. But Kobe Bryant was never one to shy away from a challenge. He entered his tenth NBA season still looking for his first scoring title. And he started out looking like a man determined to get it. Through November Bryant had scored at least 30 points in a game nine times. Then he set a career high with 62 points against the Dallas Mavericks on December 20, 2005.

That was nothing compared with what he had in store. On January 22, 2006, the Lakers hosted the Toronto Raptors. Bryant was on fire again with 26 first-half points. But the Lakers trailed by 14 at the break. Bryant decided to take it up a notch. He started launching shots from all over the court. Most of them splashed through the hoop.

Bryant scored 27 points in the third quarter and 28 more in the fourth. He ended up making 28 of 46 shots, including 7-for-13 on three-pointers. He topped it off by hitting 18-for-20 from the line. Bryant had made history with an 81-point night. It wasn't Wilt, but it was as close as anyone had ever come.

Bryant went on to win his fourth and fifth NBA titles before retiring in 2016. But his story ended in tragedy. On January 26, 2020, Bryant, his 13-year-old daughter Gianna, and seven others died in a helicopter crash in Southern California. His shocking death led to league-wide tributes. After dedicating the rest of the season to Bryant, the Lakers captured the NBA title that October.

LeBron James (23) holds the ball for a 24-second violation, in honor of Kobe Bryant's jersey number, at the start of the first Lakers' game after Bryant's death.

TIMELINE

1947

The NBL's Detroit Gems are sold to two Minnesota businessmen, who relocate the team to Minneapolis and change the name to the Lakers.

1950

George Mikan leads the Lakers to victory in the NBA Finals. The title is the Lakers' third in three years in three different leagues.

1954

The Lakers win their third straight NBA championship with a seven-game defeat of the Syracuse Nationals in the Finals.

1960

Months after the team plane survived an emergency landing in an Iowa cornfield, team owner Bob Short announces he is moving the franchise to Los Angeles.

1972

After leading the team to an NBA-record 69 victories, veterans Wilt Chamberlain and Jerry West finally deliver a championship to Los Angeles with a five-game victory over the New York Knicks.

1975

On June 16, the Lakers trade four players to the Milwaukee Bucks for future Hall of Fame center Kareem Abdul-Jabbar.

1980

On May 16, rookie Magic Johnson steps in for Abdul-Jabbar at center and scores 42 points as the Lakers clinch the NBA title with a Game 6 victory at Philadelphia.

1988

The Lakers win their fifth NBA title in nine years by knocking off the Detroit Pistons in seven games.

1991

On November 7, Johnson abruptly retires after announcing he has contracted HIV.

1996

In July the Lakers trade for Kobe Bryant and sign Shaquille O'Neal, setting the stage for the team's next dynasty.

2000

The Lakers defeat the Indiana Pacers 4–2 to capture their first title in 12 years.

2002

On June 12, O'Neal scores 34 points to lead the Lakers to a four-game sweep of the New Jersey Nets as the Lakers win their third consecutive title.

2006

On January 22, Bryant scores 81 points in a home game against the Toronto Raptors. It is the second-highest-scoring game in NBA history.

2010

On June 17, Bryant scores 23 points and grabs 15 rebounds to lift the Lakers past the Celtics 83–79 in Game 7 of the NBA Finals. It's the team's second straight title and the record eleventh championship for coach Phil Jackson.

2018

Superstar forward LeBron James signs a free agent contract with the Lakers. He leads the team to another title in his second season.

2020

On January 26, Bryant dies in a helicopter crash. On October 11, the Lakers close out the Miami Heat to win a COVID-delayed NBA Finals in Orlando, Florida.

TEAM FACTS

FRANCHISE HISTORY

Minneapolis Lakers (1947–60),
Los Angeles Lakers (1960–)

NBA CHAMPIONSHIPS

1949, 1950, 1952, 1953, 1954, 1972, 1980, 1982, 1985, 1987, 1988, 2000, 2001, 2002, 2009, 2010, 2020

KEY PLAYERS

Kareem Abdul-Jabbar (1975–89)
Elgin Baylor (1958–71)
Kobe Bryant (1996–2016)
Wilt Chamberlain (1968–73)
Anthony Davis (2019–)
LeBron James (2018–)
Earvin "Magic" Johnson (1979–91, 1996)
George Mikan (1947–54, 1956)
Vern Mikkelsen (1949–59)
Shaquille O'Neal (1996–2004)
Jerry West (1960–74)
James Worthy (1982–94)

KEY COACHES

Phil Jackson (1999–04, 2005–11)
John Kundla (1947–57, 1958–59)
Pat Riley (1981–90)

HOME ARENAS

Minneapolis Auditorium (1947–60)
Los Angeles Memorial Sports Arena (1960–67)
The Great Western Forum (1967–99)
Known as:
The Forum (1967–88)
Crypto.com Arena (1999–)
Formerly known as:
Staples Center (1999–2021)

TEAM TRIVIA

BEST BUD

Bud Grant was a reserve forward on the Lakers' first two NBA title teams in 1950 and 1951. He averaged just 2.6 points per game. But Grant was also an excellent football player. After a professional football career in both the United States and Canada, he became the head coach of the Minnesota Vikings. He led the Vikings to 158 wins and four Super Bowl appearances in 18 years on the sideline.

LAS VEGAS SCORE

Kareem Abdul-Jabbar broke Wilt Chamberlain's NBA scoring record on April 5, 1984, against the Utah Jazz. Oddly, the game was played in a city that does not have an NBA team—Las Vegas. The Jazz played 11 home games in the Nevada city during the 1983–84 season. Abdul-Jabbar's record-breaking moment just happened to take place during one of them.

ICONIC COLOR

While the Lakers played in Minneapolis, their main colors were powder blue or royal blue. They kept those colors when they moved to Los Angeles. But when they began playing in the Forum in 1967, they decided to change to purple and gold. Legend has it, Lakers announcer Chick Hearn referred to the shade of purple as "Forum Blue" and the name stuck.

GLOSSARY

assist
A pass that leads directly to a basket.

double-double
Accumulating 10 or more of two certain statistics in a game.

draft
A system that allows teams to acquire new players coming into a league.

elite
The best of the best.

franchise
A sports organization, including the top-level team and all minor league affiliates.

goaltending
Interfering with a ball on the way to the basket when it's on the way down or directly above the rim.

iconic
Widely recognized or acknowledged as a representation of a larger organization.

layup
A shot made from close to the basket; an easy shot.

merge
Join to form a new entity.

outlet pass
A quick pass made up the court after a player grabs a rebound; usually starts a fast break.

rebound
To catch the ball after a shot has been missed.

rookie
A professional athlete in his or her first year of competition.

triple-double
Accumulating 10 or more of three certain statistics in a game.

versatility
The ability to perform many different roles or functions.

MORE INFORMATION

BOOKS

Flynn, Brendan. *The NBA Encyclopedia for Kids*. Minneapolis, MN: Abdo Publishing, 2022.

Gagne, Tammy. *Kobe Bryant: Basketball Superstar*. Minneapolis, MN: Abdo Publishing, 2021.

Murray, Laura K. *LeBron James: NBA Champion*. Minneapolis, MN: Abdo Publishing, 2020.

ONLINE RESOURCES

To learn more about the Los Angeles Lakers, please visit **abdobooklinks.com** or scan this QR code. These links are routinely monitored and updated to provide the most current information available.

INDEX

ABOUT THE AUTHOR

Patrick Donnelly is a freelance writer who lives in Minneapolis, Minnesota. He has covered the NBA for 20 years.